MznLnx

Missing Links Exam Preps

Exam Prep for

Basic Mathematics

Bittinger, 10th Edition

The MznLnx Exam Prep is your link from the texbook and lecture to your exams.
The MznLnx Exam Preps are unauthorized and comprehensive reviews of your textbooks.

All material provided by MznLnx and Rico Publications (c) 2010
Textbook publishers and textbook authors do not particpate in or contribute to these reviews.

MznLnx

Rico
Publications

Exam Prep for Basic Mathematics
10th Edition
Bittinger

Publisher: Raymond Houge
Assistant Editor: Michael Rouger
Text and Cover Designer: Lisa Buckner
Marketing Manager: Sara Swagger
Project Manager, Editorial Production: Jerry Emerson
Art Director: Vernon Lowerui

Product Manager: Dave Mason
Editorial Assitant: Rachel Guzmanji
Pedagogy: Debra Long
Cover Image: Jim Reed/Getty Images
Text and Cover Printer: City Printing, Inc.
Compositor: Media Mix, Inc.

(c) 2010 Rico Publications

ALL RIGHTS RESERVED. No part of this work covered by the copyright may be reproduced or used in any form or by an means--graphic, electronic, or mechanical, including photocopying, recording, taping, Web distribution, information storage, and retrieval systems, or in any other manner--without the written permission of the publisher.

For more information about our products, contact us at:
Dave.Mason@RicoPublications.com

For permission to use material from this text or product, submit a request online to:
Dave.Mason@RicoPublications.com

Printed in the United States
ISBN:

Contents

CHAPTER 1
WHOLE NUMBERS — 1

CHAPTER 2
FRACTION NOTATION: MULTIPLICATION AND DIVISION — 14

CHAPTER 3
FRACTION NOTATION AND MIXED NUMERALS — 19

CHAPTER 4
DECIMAL NOTATION — 25

CHAPTER 5
RATIO AND PROPORTION — 30

CHAPTER 6
PERCENT NOTATION — 36

CHAPTER 7
DATA, GRAPHS, AND STATISTICS — 40

CHAPTER 8
MEASUREMENT — 46

CHAPTER 9
GEOMETRY — 51

CHAPTER 10
REAL NUMBERS — 62

CHAPTER 11
ALGEBRA: SOLVING EQUATIONS AND PROBLEMS — 68

ANSWER KEY — 74

TO THE STUDENT

COMPREHENSIVE

The *MznLnx* Exam Prep series is designed to help you pass your exams. Editors at MznLnx review your textbooks and then prepare these practice exams to help you master the textbook material. Unlike study guides, workbooks, and practice tests provided by the texbook publisher and textbook authors, *MznLnx* gives you **all** of the material in each chapter in exam form, not just samples, so you can be sure to nail your exam.

MECHANICAL

The MznLnx Exam Prep series creates exams that will help you learn the subject matter as well as test you on your understanding. Each question is designed to help you master the concept. Just working through the exams, you gain an understanding of the subject--its a simple mechanical process that produces success.

INTEGRATED STUDY GUIDE AND REVIEW

MznLnx is not just a set of exams designed to test you, its also a comprehensive review of the subject content. Each exam question is also a review of the concept, making sure that you will get the answer correct without having to go to other sources of material. You learn as you go! Its the easiest way to pass an exam.

HUMOR

Studying can be tedious and dry. MznLnx's instructional design includes moderate humor within the exam questions on occassion, to break the tedium and revitalize the brain

Chapter 1. WHOLE NUMBERS

1. In mathematics, the _____ is a term used to describe the number of times one must apply a given operation to an integer before reaching a fixed point.

Usually, this refers to the additive or multiplicative persistence of an integer, which is how often one has to replace the number by the sum or product of its digits until one reaches a single digit. Because the numbers are broken down into their digits, the additive or multiplicative persistence depends on the radix.

   a. Coprime
   b. Persistence of a number
   c. Linear congruence theorem
   d. Lychrel number

2. In mathematics, a _____ is a number that can be expressed as an integral of an algebraic function over an algebraic domain. Kontsevich and Zagier define a _____ as a complex number whose real and imaginary parts are values of absolutely convergent integrals of rational functions with rational coefficients, over domains in given by polynomial inequalities with rational coefficients.
   a. Boussinesq approximation
   b. Period
   c. Closeness
   d. Disk

3. _____ is a numeral system in which each position is related to the next by a constant multiplier, a common ratio, called the base or radix of that numeral system.
   a. Cyrillic numerals
   b. NegaFibonacci coding
   c. Negative base
   d. Place value

4. In mathematics, a _____ can mean either an element of the set {1, 2, 3, ...} or an element of the set {0, 1, 2, 3, ...}. The latter is especially preferred in mathematical logic, set theory, and computer science.

_____s have two main purposes: they can be used for counting, and they can be used for ordering.

   a. Strong partition cardinal
   b. Natural number
   c. Cardinal numbers
   d. Suslin cardinal

Chapter 1. WHOLE NUMBERS

5. In mathematics, a _____ can mean either an element of the set {1, 2, 3, ...} (i.e the positive integers) or an element of the set {0, 1, 2, 3, ...} (i.e. the non-negative integers).
   a. Degrees of freedom
   b. FISH
   c. Bounded
   d. Whole number

6. In mathematics the concept of a _____ generalizes notions such as 'length', 'area', and 'volume'. Informally, given some base set, a '_____' is any consistent assignment of 'sizes' to the subsets of the base set. Depending on the application, the 'size' of a subset may be interpreted as its physical size, the amount of something that lies within the subset, or the probability that some random process will yield a result within the subset.
   a. Lattice
   b. Cusp
   c. Congruent
   d. Measure

7. An _____ is a number which is involved in addition. A number being added is considered to be an _____.
   a. A Mathematical Theory of Communication
   b. A posteriori
   c. A chemical equation
   d. Addend

8. In mathematics the _____ of a set which is equipped with the operation of addition is an element which, when added to any element x in the set, yields x. One of the most familiar additive identities is the number 0 from elementary mathematics, but additive identities occur in other mathematical structures where addition is defined, such as in groups and rings.

   - The _____ familiar from elementary mathematics is zero, denoted 0. For example,

   $5 + 0 = 5 = 0 + 5.$

   - In the natural numbers N and all of its supersets, the _____ is 0. Thus for any one of these numbers n,

   $n + 0 = n = 0 + n.$

Let N be a set which is closed under the operation of addition, denoted +. An _____ for N is any element e such that for any element n in N,

$e + n = n = n + e.$

a. Unique factorization domain
b. Additive identity
c. Algebraically independent
d. Unit ring

9. In mathematics, _____ is a property that a binary operation can have. It means that, within an expression containing two or more of the same associative operators in a row, the order that the operations are performed does not matter as long as the sequence of the operands is not changed. That is, rearranging the parentheses in such an expression will not change its value.
   a. Algebraically closed
   b. Unital
   c. Associativity
   d. Idempotence

10. The _____ is a rule which states that when you add or multiply numbers, changing the order doesn't change the result.
    a. Commutative law
    b. Coimage
    c. Conditional event algebra
    d. Semigroupoid

11. In mathematics, the term _____ has several different important meanings:

    - An _____ is an equality that remains true regardless of the values of any variables that appear within it, to distinguish it from an equality which is true under more particular conditions. For this, the 'triple bar' symbol ≡ is sometimes used.
    - In algebra, an _____ or _____ element of a set S with a binary operation Â· is an element e that, when combined with any element x of S, produces that same x. That is, eÂ·x = xÂ·e = x for all x in S.
        o The _____ function from a set S to itself, often denoted id or id$_S$, s the function such that i = x for all x in S. This function serves as the _____ element in the set of all functions from S to itself with respect to function composition.
        o In linear algebra, the _____ matrix of size n is the n-by-n square matrix with ones on the main diagonal and zeros elsewhere. This matrix serves as the _____ with respect to matrix multiplication.

A common example of the first meaning is the trigonometric _____

$$\sin^2 \theta + \cos^2 \theta = 1$$

which is true for all real values of θ, as opposed to

$$\cos\theta = 1,$$

which is true only for some values of θ, not all. For example, the latter equation is true when $\theta = 0$, false when $\theta = 2$

The concepts of 'additive _____' and 'multiplicative _____' are central to the Peano axioms. The number 0 is the 'additive _____' for integers, real numbers, and complex numbers. For the real numbers, for all $a \in \mathbb{R}$,

$$0 + a = a,$$

$$a + 0 = a,\text{ and}$$

$$0 + 0 = 0.$$

Similarly, The number 1 is the 'multiplicative _____' for integers, real numbers, and complex numbers.

a. Intersection
b. Action
c. ARIA
d. Identity

12. The _____ is the length of the line that bounds an area In the special case where the area is circular, the _____ is known as the circumference.

a. Perimeter
b. Multilateration
c. Reflection symmetry
d. Concyclic

13. A _____ is a device for performing mathematical calculations, distinguished from a computer by having a limited problem solving ability and an interface optimized for interactive calculation rather than programming. _____s can be hardware or software, and mechanical or electronic, and are often built into devices such as PDAs or mobile phones.

Modern electronic _____s are generally small, digital, and usually inexpensive.

Chapter 1. WHOLE NUMBERS

a. Calculator
b. 1-center problem
c. 2-3 heap
d. 120-cell

14. The traditional names for the parts of the formula c − b = a, are _____ (c) − subtrahend (b) = difference (a). The words _____ and subtrahend are uncommon in modern usage. Instead we say that c and −b are terms, and treat subtraction as addition of the opposite. The answer is still called the difference.
    a. Minuend
    b. Plus and minus signs
    c. Multiplication
    d. Lowest common denominator

15. The quantity that is deducted from the minuend in subtraction is the _____.
    a. The number 0 is even.
    b. Subtrahend
    c. Lowest common denominator
    d. Trailing zeros

16. In mathematics, the _____ of a number n is the number that, when added to n, yields zero. The _____ of n is denoted −n. For example, 7 is −7, because 7 + (−7) = 0, and the _____ of −0.3 is 0.3, because −0.3 + 0.3 = 0.
    a. Arity
    b. Associativity
    c. Algebraic structure
    d. Additive inverse

17. _____ involves reducing the number of significant digits in a number. The result of _____ is a 'shorter' number having fewer non-zero digits yet similar in magnitude. The result is less precise but easier to use.
    a. Shabakh
    b. Hyper operator
    c. Sudan function
    d. Rounding

18. In mathematics, an inequality is a statement about the relative size or order of two objects. For example 14 > 10, or 14 is _____ 10. The notation a > b means that a is _____ b and 'a' would be to the right of 'b' on a number line.

a. Greater than
b. Cauchy-Schwarz inequality
c. FKG inequality
d. Minkowski inequality

19. In mathematics, an _____ is a statement about the relative size or order of two objects, or about whether they are the same or not

- The notation a < b means that a is less than b.
- The notation a > b means that a is greater than b.
- The notation a ≠ b means that a is not equal to b, but does not say that one is bigger than the other or even that they can be compared in size.

In all these cases, a is not equal to b, hence, '_____'.

These relations are known as strict _____

- The notation a ≤ b means that a is less than or equal to b;
- The notation a ≥ b means that a is greater than or equal to b;

An additional use of the notation is to show that one quantity is much greater than another, normally by several orders of magnitude.

- The notation a << b means that a is much less than b.
- The notation a >> b means that a is much greater than b.

If the sense of the _____ is the same for all values of the variables for which its members are defined, then the _____ is called an 'absolute' or 'unconditional' _____. If the sense of an _____ holds only for certain values of the variables involved, but is reversed or destroyed for other values of the variables, it is called a conditional _____.

An _____ may appear unsolvable because it only states whether a number is larger or smaller than another number; but it is possible to apply the same operations for equalities to inequalities. For example, to find x for the _____ 10x > 23 one would divide 23 by 10.

a. A posteriori
b. Inequality
c. A Mathematical Theory of Communication
d. A chemical equation

Chapter 1. WHOLE NUMBERS

20. The _____ is a decimalised system of measurement. It exists in several variations, with different choices of base units, though the choice of base units does not affect its day-to-day use. Over the last two centuries, different variants have been considered the _____.

    a. George Dantzig
    b. Nonlinear system
    c. 1-center problem
    d. Metric system

21. In mathematics, an _____ in the sense of ring theory is a subring $\mathcal{O}$ of a ring R that satisfies the conditions

    1. R is a ring which is a finite-dimensional algebra over the rational number field $\mathbb{Q}$
    2. $\mathcal{O}$ spans R over $\mathbb{Q}$, so that $\mathbb{Q}\mathcal{O} = R$, and
    3. $\mathcal{O}$ is a lattice in R.

    The third condition can be stated more accurately, in terms of the extension of scalars of R to the real numbers, embedding R in a real vector space. In less formal terms, additively $\mathcal{O}$ should be a free abelian group generated by a basis for R over $\mathbb{Q}$.

    The leading example is the case where R is a number field K and $\mathcal{O}$ is its ring of integers. In algebraic number theory there are examples for any K other than the rational field of proper subrings of the ring of integers that are also _____s.

    a. Efficiency
    b. Annihilator
    c. Order
    d. Algebraic

22. A _____ is a software program that facilitates symbolic mathematics. The core functionality of a CAS is manipulation of mathematical expressions in symbolic form.

The symbolic manipulations supported typically include

- simplification to the smallest possible expression or some standard form, including automatic simplification with assumptions and simplification with constraints
- substitution of symbolic, functors or numeric values for expressions
- change of form of expressions: expanding products and powers, partial and full factorization, rewriting as partial fractions, constraint satisfaction, rewriting trigonometric functions as exponentials, etc.
- partial and total differentiation
- symbolic constrained and unconstrained global optimization
- solution of linear and some non-linear equations over various domains
- solution of some differential and difference equations
- taking some limits
- some indefinite and definite integration, including multidimensional integrals
- integral transforms
- arbitrary-precision numeric operations
- Series operations such as expansion, summation and products
- matrix operations including products, inverses, etc.
- display of mathematical expressions in two-dimensional mathematical form, often using typesetting systems similar to TeX
- add-ons for use in applied mathematics such as physics packages for physical computation
- plotting graphs and parametric plots of functions in two and three dimensions, and animating them
- APIs for linking it on an external program such as a database, or using in a programming language to use the _____
- drawing charts and diagrams
- string manipulation such as matching and searching
- statistical computation
- Theorem proving and verification
- graphic production and editing such as CGI and signal processing as image processing
- sound synthesis

Many also include a programming language, allowing users to implement their own algorithms.

Some _____s focus on a specific area of application; these are typically developed in academia and are free.

a. 1-center problem
b. 120-cell
c. Computer algebra system
d. 2-3 heap

Chapter 1. WHOLE NUMBERS

23. In computer science an _____ is a data structure consisting of a group of elements that are accessed by indexing. In most programming languages each element has the same data type and the _____ occupies a contiguous area of storage.

Most programming languages have a built-in _____ data type, although what is called an _____ in the language documentation is sometimes really an associative _____.

a. A chemical equation
b. A Mathematical Theory of Communication
c. A posteriori
d. Array

24. _____ is the mathematical operation of scaling one number by another. It is one of the four basic operations in elementary arithmetic.

_____ is defined for whole numbers in terms of repeated addition; for example, 4 multiplied by 3 can be calculated by adding 3 copies of 4 together:

$$4 + 4 + 4 = 12.$$

_____ of rational numbers and real numbers is defined by systematic generalization of this basic idea.

a. The number 0 is even.
b. Least common multiple
c. Highest common factor
d. Multiplication

25. In abstract algebra, a field extension L /K is called _____ if every element of L is _____ over K. Field extensions which are not _____.

For example, the field extension R/Q, that is the field of real numbers as an extension of the field of rational numbers, is transcendental, while the field extensions C/R and Q

a. Algebraic
b. Ideal
c. Echo
d. Identity

26. In mathematics, and in particular in abstract algebra, distributivity is a property of binary operations that generalises the _____ law from elementary algebra.
   a. General linear group
   b. Permutation
   c. Closure with a twist
   d. Distributive

27. _____ is a quantity expressing the two-dimensional size of a defined part of a surface, typically a region bounded by a closed curve. The term surface _____ refers to the total _____ of the exposed surface of a 3-dimensional solid, such as the sum of the _____s of the exposed sides of a polyhedron. _____ is an important invariant in the differential geometry of surfaces.
   a. A Mathematical Theory of Communication
   b. A chemical equation
   c. A posteriori
   d. Area

28. In geometry, a _____ is defined as a quadrilateral where all four of its angles are right angles.
   a. Cantor-Dedekind axiom
   b. Polytope
   c. Point group in two dimensions
   d. Rectangle

29. _____s are payments made by a corporation to its shareholder members. When a corporation earns a profit or surplus, that money can be put to two uses: it can either be re-invested in the business, or it can be paid to the shareholders as a _____. Many corporations retain a portion of their earnings and pay the remainder as a _____.
   a. GNU Privacy Guard
   b. 1-center problem
   c. 120-cell
   d. Dividend

30. In mathematics, a _____ of an integer n is an integer which evenly divides n without leaving a remainder.

For example, 7 is a _____ of 42 because 42/7 = 6. We also say 42 is divisible by 7 or 42 is a multiple of 7 or 7 divides 42 or 7 is a factor of 42 and we usually write 7 | 42.

a. Divisor
b. 2-3 heap
c. 120-cell
d. 1-center problem

31. In mathematics, a _____ is the end result of a division problem. It can also be expressed as the number of times the divisor divides into the dividend.
    a. Marginal cost
    b. Notation
    c. Limiting
    d. Quotient

32. In mathematics, a division is called a _____ if the divisor is zero. Such a division can be formally expressed as $\frac{a}{0}$ where a is the dividend. Whether this expression can be assigned a well-defined value depends upon the mathematical setting.
    a. 120-cell
    b. 1-center problem
    c. Division by Zero
    d. 2-3 heap

33. In the mathematical discipline of graph theory, a graph labeling is the assignment of labels, traditionally represented with integers, to the edges or vertices of a graph.

Formally, given a graph G: = with V being the set of vertices and E being the set of edges, a vertex labeling is a function from some subset of the integers to the verticies of the graph. A graph with such function defined is called a vertex-_____.

   a. 1-center problem
   b. 120-cell
   c. 2-3 heap
   d. Labeled graph

34. A _____ is a deliberate process for transforming one or more inputs into one or more results, with variable change.

The term is used in a variety of senses, from the very definite arithmetical using an algorithm to the vague heuristics of calculating a strategy in a competition or calculating the chance of a successful relationship between two people.

Multiplying 7 by 8 is a simple algorithmic _____.

  a. Mathematical maturity
  b. Calculation
  c. Mathematics Subject Classification
  d. Mathematical object

35. In mathematics and computer science, _____ (also base-16, hexa or base, of 16. It uses sixteen distinct symbols, most often the symbols 0-9 to represent values zero to nine, and A, B, C, D, E, F (or a through f) to represent values ten to fifteen.

Its primary use is as a human friendly representation of binary coded values, so it is often used in digital electronics and computer engineering.

  a. Radix
  b. Hexadecimal
  c. Factoradic
  d. Tetradecimal

36. Exponentiation is a mathematical operation, written a^n, involving two numbers, the base a and the _____ n. When n is a positive integer, exponentiation corresponds to repeated multiplication:

$$a^n = \underbrace{a \times \cdots \times a}_{n},$$

just as multiplication by a positive integer corresponds to repeated addition:

$$a \times n = \underbrace{a + \cdots + a}_{n}.$$

The _____ is usually shown as a superscript to the right of the base. The exponentiation a^n can be read as: a raised to the n-th power, a raised to the power [of] n or possibly a raised to the _____ [of] n, or more briefly: a to the n-th power or a to the power [of] n, or even more briefly: a to the n.

a. Exponent
b. Exponential sum
c. Exponentiating by squaring
d. Exponential tree

37. Scientific notation, also sometimes known as standard form or as _____, is a way of writing numbers that accommodates values too large or small to be conveniently written in standard decimal notation. Scientific notation has a number of useful properties and is often favored by scientists, mathematicians and engineers, who work with such numbers.

In scientific notation, numbers are written in the form:

$$a \times 10^b$$

a. A chemical equation
b. A Mathematical Theory of Communication
c. Exponential notation
d. A posteriori

38. In algebra and computer programming, when a number or expression is both preceded and followed by a binary operation, a rule is required for which operation should be applied first; this rule is known as an _____ . From the earliest use of mathematical notation, multiplication took precedence over addition, whichever side of a number it appeared on. Thus 3 + 4 × 5 = 5 × 4 + 3 = 23.
a. Algebraic K-theory
b. Isomorphism class
c. Identity element
d. Order of operations

39. In mathematics, an _____, or central tendency of a data set refers to a measure of the 'middle' or 'expected' value of the data set. There are many different descriptive statistics that can be chosen as a measurement of the central tendency of the data items.

An _____ is a single value that is meant to typify a list of values.

a. A chemical equation
b. A posteriori
c. Average
d. A Mathematical Theory of Communication

Chapter 2. FRACTION NOTATION: MULTIPLICATION AND DIVISION

1. In mathematics, a _____ can mean either an element of the set {1, 2, 3, ...} or an element of the set {0, 1, 2, 3, ...}. The latter is especially preferred in mathematical logic, set theory, and computer science.

   _____s have two main purposes: they can be used for counting, and they can be used for ordering.

   a. Strong partition cardinal
   b. Natural number
   c. Suslin cardinal
   d. Cardinal numbers

2. A _____ is a device for performing mathematical calculations, distinguished from a computer by having a limited problem solving ability and an interface optimized for interactive calculation rather than programming. _____s can be hardware or software, and mechanical or electronic, and are often built into devices such as PDAs or mobile phones.

   Modern electronic _____s are generally small, digital, and usually inexpensive.

   a. 1-center problem
   b. 120-cell
   c. 2-3 heap
   d. Calculator

3. In mathematics, a _____ can mean either an element of the set {1, 2, 3, ...} (i.e the positive integers) or an element of the set {0, 1, 2, 3, ...} (i.e. the non-negative integers).
   a. Bounded
   b. FISH
   c. Whole number
   d. Degrees of freedom

4. A _____ number is a positive integer which has a positive divisor other than one or itself. By definition, every integer greater than one is either a prime number or a _____ number. zero and one are considered to be neither prime nor _____. For example, the integer 14 is a _____ number because it can be factored as 2 × 7.
   a. Key server
   b. Discontinuity
   c. Basis
   d. Composite

5. A _____ is a positive integer which has a positive divisor other than one or itself. In other words, if 0 < n is an integer and there are integers 1 < a, b < n such that n = a × b then n is composite. By definition, every integer greater than one is either a prime number or a _____.

Chapter 2. FRACTION NOTATION: MULTIPLICATION AND DIVISION

a. Megaprime
b. Prime Pages
c. Ruth-Aaron pair
d. Composite number

6. In mathematics, a _____ is a natural number which has exactly two distinct natural number divisors: 1 and itself. An infinitude of _____s exists, as demonstrated by Euclid around 300 BC. The first twenty-five _____s are:

2, 3, 5, 7, 11, 13, 17, 19, 23, 29, 31, 37, 41, 43, 47, 53, 59, 61, 67, 71, 73, 79, 83, 89, 97.

a. Pronic number
b. Perrin number
c. Highly composite number
d. Prime number

7. In set theory, a _____ is a partially ordered set such that for each $t \in T$, the set $\{s \in T : s < t\}$ is well-ordered by the relation $<$. For each $t \in T$, the order type of $\{s \in T : s < t\}$ is called the height of t. The height of T itself is the least ordinal greater than the height of each element of T.

a. Tree
b. Set-theoretic topology
c. Definable numbers
d. Transitive reduction

8. _____ is the mathematical operation of scaling one number by another. It is one of the four basic operations in elementary arithmetic.

_____ is defined for whole numbers in terms of repeated addition; for example, 4 multiplied by 3 can be calculated by adding 3 copies of 4 together:

$$4 + 4 + 4 = 12.$$

_____ of rational numbers and real numbers is defined by systematic generalization of this basic idea.

a. The number 0 is even.
b. Least common multiple
c. Highest common factor
d. Multiplication

Chapter 2. FRACTION NOTATION: MULTIPLICATION AND DIVISION

9. In abstract algebra, a field extension L /K is called _____ if every element of L is _____ over K. Field extensions which are not _____.

For example, the field extension R/Q, that is the field of real numbers as an extension of the field of rational numbers, is transcendental, while the field extensions C/R and Q

   a. Echo
   b. Algebraic
   c. Identity
   d. Ideal

10. In the study of metric spaces in mathematics, there are various notions of two metrics on the same underlying space being 'the same', or _____.

In the following, M will denote a non-empty set and d_1 and d_2 will denote two metrics on M.

The two metrics d_1 and d_2 are said to be topologically _____ if they generate the same topology on M.

   a. A chemical equation
   b. A Mathematical Theory of Communication
   c. Equivalent
   d. A posteriori

11. In mathematics, the term _____ has several different important meanings:

   - An _____ is an equality that remains true regardless of the values of any variables that appear within it, to distinguish it from an equality which is true under more particular conditions. For this, the 'triple bar' symbol ≡ is sometimes used.
   - In algebra, an _____ or _____ element of a set S with a binary operation Â· is an element e that, when combined with any element x of S, produces that same x. That is, eÂ·x = xÂ·e = x for all x in S.
     o The _____ function from a set S to itself, often denoted id or id_S, s the function such that i = x for all x in S. This function serves as the _____ element in the set of all functions from S to itself with respect to function composition.
     o In linear algebra, the _____ matrix of size n is the n-by-n square matrix with ones on the main diagonal and zeros elsewhere. This matrix serves as the _____ with respect to matrix multiplication.

A common example of the first meaning is the trigonometric _____

$$\sin^2 \theta + \cos^2 \theta = 1$$

Chapter 2. FRACTION NOTATION: MULTIPLICATION AND DIVISION

which is true for all real values of θ, as opposed to

$$\cos\theta = 1,$$

which is true only for some values of θ, not all. For example, the latter equation is true when $\theta = 0$, false when $\theta = 2$

The concepts of 'additive _____' and 'multiplicative _____' are central to the Peano axioms. The number 0 is the 'additive _____' for integers, real numbers, and complex numbers. For the real numbers, for all $a \in \mathbb{R}$,

$$0 + a = a,$$

$$a + 0 = a, \text{ and}$$

$$0 + 0 = 0.$$

Similarly, The number 1 is the 'multiplicative _____' for integers, real numbers, and complex numbers.

a. ARIA
b. Action
c. Identity
d. Intersection

12. In mathematics, the _____ or least common denominator is the least common multiple of the denominators of a set of vulgar fractions. It is the smallest positive integer that is a multiple of the denominators. For instance, the _____ of

$$\left\{\frac{5}{12}, \frac{11}{18}\right\}$$

is 36 because the least common multiple of 12 and 18 is 36.

a. The number 0 is even.
b. Highest common factor
c. Subtrahend
d. Lowest common denominator

Chapter 2. FRACTION NOTATION: MULTIPLICATION AND DIVISION

13. In mathematics the concept of a _____ generalizes notions such as 'length', 'area', and 'volume'. Informally, given some base set, a '_____' is any consistent assignment of 'sizes' to the subsets of the base set. Depending on the application, the 'size' of a subset may be interpreted as its physical size, the amount of something that lies within the subset, or the probability that some random process will yield a result within the subset.
    a. Congruent
    b. Lattice
    c. Cusp
    d. Measure

14. In mathematics, the multiplicative inverse of a number x, denoted 1/x or x^{-1}, is the number which, when multiplied by x, yields 1. The multiplicative inverse of x is also called the _____ of x.
    a. 1-center problem
    b. 120-cell
    c. 2-3 heap
    d. Reciprocal

15. In the mathematical discipline of graph theory, a graph labeling is the assignment of labels, traditionally represented with integers, to the edges or vertices of a graph.

    Formally, given a graph G: = with V being the set of vertices and E being the set of edges, a vertex labeling is a function from some subset of the integers to the verticies of the graph. A graph with such function defined is called a vertex-_____.

    a. 1-center problem
    b. Labeled graph
    c. 2-3 heap
    d. 120-cell

16. A _____ is a word, phrase, number or other sequence of units that can be read the same way in either direction. Composing literature in _____s is an example of constrained writing. The word '_____' was coined from Greek roots palin and dromos by English writer Ben Jonson in the 1600s.
    a. Metalanguage
    b. 1-center problem
    c. Palindrome
    d. 120-cell

Chapter 3. FRACTION NOTATION AND MIXED NUMERALS

1. In arithmetic and number theory, the _____ or lowest common multiple or smallest common multiple of two integers a and b is the smallest positive integer that is a multiple of both a and b. Since it is a multiple, it can be divided by a and b without a remainder. If either a or b is 0, so that there is no such positive integer, then lc is defined to be zero.

    a. Lowest common denominator
    b. Least common multiple
    c. Plus-minus sign
    d. Plus and minus signs

2. In mathematics the concept of a _____ generalizes notions such as 'length', 'area', and 'volume'. Informally, given some base set, a '_____' is any consistent assignment of 'sizes' to the subsets of the base set. Depending on the application, the 'size' of a subset may be interpreted as its physical size, the amount of something that lies within the subset, or the probability that some random process will yield a result within the subset.

    a. Congruent
    b. Cusp
    c. Lattice
    d. Measure

3. In mathematics, a _____ is a natural number which has exactly two distinct natural number divisors: 1 and itself. An infinitude of _____s exists, as demonstrated by Euclid around 300 BC. The first twenty-five _____s are:

    2, 3, 5, 7, 11, 13, 17, 19, 23, 29, 31, 37, 41, 43, 47, 53, 59, 61, 67, 71, 73, 79, 83, 89, 97.

    a. Perrin number
    b. Pronic number
    c. Highly composite number
    d. Prime number

4. In mathematics, a _____ can mean either an element of the set {1, 2, 3, ...} or an element of the set {0, 1, 2, 3, ...}. The latter is especially preferred in mathematical logic, set theory, and computer science.

    _____s have two main purposes: they can be used for counting, and they can be used for ordering.

    a. Cardinal numbers
    b. Suslin cardinal
    c. Strong partition cardinal
    d. Natural number

Chapter 3. FRACTION NOTATION AND MIXED NUMERALS

5. Scientific notation, also sometimes known as standard form or as _____, is a way of writing numbers that accommodates values too large or small to be conveniently written in standard decimal notation. Scientific notation has a number of useful properties and is often favored by scientists, mathematicians and engineers, who work with such numbers.

In scientific notation, numbers are written in the form:

$$a \times 10^b$$

a. Exponential notation
b. A Mathematical Theory of Communication
c. A posteriori
d. A chemical equation

6. An _____ is a number which is involved in addition. A number being added is considered to be an _____.
a. Addend
b. A chemical equation
c. A Mathematical Theory of Communication
d. A posteriori

7. In mathematics, the _____ or least common denominator is the least common multiple of the denominators of a set of vulgar fractions. It is the smallest positive integer that is a multiple of the denominators. For instance, the _____ of

$$\left\{\frac{5}{12}, \frac{11}{18}\right\}$$

is 36 because the least common multiple of 12 and 18 is 36.

a. Highest common factor
b. Lowest common denominator
c. The number 0 is even.
d. Subtrahend

8. _____ is the mathematical operation of scaling one number by another. It is one of the four basic operations in elementary arithmetic.

Chapter 3. FRACTION NOTATION AND MIXED NUMERALS

_____ is defined for whole numbers in terms of repeated addition; for example, 4 multiplied by 3 can be calculated by adding 3 copies of 4 together:

$$4 + 4 + 4 = 12.$$

_____ of rational numbers and real numbers is defined by systematic generalization of this basic idea.

a. The number 0 is even.
b. Least common multiple
c. Highest common factor
d. Multiplication

9. In abstract algebra, a field extension L /K is called _____ if every element of L is _____ over K. Field extensions which are not _____.

For example, the field extension R/Q, that is the field of real numbers as an extension of the field of rational numbers, is transcendental, while the field extensions C/R and Q

a. Algebraic
b. Ideal
c. Echo
d. Identity

10. In mathematics, the _____ of a number n is the number that, when added to n, yields zero. The _____ of n is denoted −n. For example, 7 is −7, because 7 + (−7) = 0, and the _____ of −0.3 is 0.3, because −0.3 + 0.3 = 0.

a. Additive inverse
b. Algebraic structure
c. Arity
d. Associativity

11. In mathematics, an _____ in the sense of ring theory is a subring $\mathcal{O}$ of a ring R that satisfies the conditions

1. R is a ring which is a finite-dimensional algebra over the rational number field $\mathbb{Q}$
2. $\mathcal{O}$ spans R over $\mathbb{Q}$, so that $\mathbb{Q}\mathcal{O} = R$, and
3. $\mathcal{O}$ is a lattice in R.

22   *Chapter 3. FRACTION NOTATION AND MIXED NUMERALS*

The third condition can be stated more accurately, in terms of the extension of scalars of R to the real numbers, embedding R in a real vector space. In less formal terms, additively $\mathcal{O}$ should be a free abelian group generated by a basis for R over $\mathbb{Q}$.

The leading example is the case where R is a number field K and $\mathcal{O}$ is its ring of integers. In algebraic number theory there are examples for any K other than the rational field of proper subrings of the ring of integers that are also _____s.

   a. Algebraic
   b. Efficiency
   c. Annihilator
   d. Order

12. In the mathematical discipline of graph theory, a graph labeling is the assignment of labels, traditionally represented with integers, to the edges or vertices of a graph.

Formally, given a graph G: = with V being the set of vertices and E being the set of edges, a vertex labeling is a function from some subset of the integers to the verticies of the graph. A graph with such function defined is called a vertex-_____.

   a. 1-center problem
   b. 2-3 heap
   c. 120-cell
   d. Labeled graph

13. In mathematics, a _____ is the end result of a division problem. It can also be expressed as the number of times the divisor divides into the dividend.
   a. Quotient
   b. Limiting
   c. Notation
   d. Marginal cost

14. A _____ is a device for performing mathematical calculations, distinguished from a computer by having a limited problem solving ability and an interface optimized for interactive calculation rather than programming. _____s can be hardware or software, and mechanical or electronic, and are often built into devices such as PDAs or mobile phones.

Modern electronic _____s are generally small, digital, and usually inexpensive.

Chapter 3. FRACTION NOTATION AND MIXED NUMERALS

a. 120-cell
b. 2-3 heap
c. 1-center problem
d. Calculator

15. In mathematics, a _____ can mean either an element of the set {1, 2, 3, ...} (i.e the positive integers) or an element of the set {0, 1, 2, 3, ...} (i.e. the non-negative integers).
   a. FISH
   b. Bounded
   c. Whole number
   d. Degrees of freedom

16. In algebra and computer programming, when a number or expression is both preceded and followed by a binary operation, a rule is required for which operation should be applied first; this rule is known as an _____ . From the earliest use of mathematical notation, multiplication took precedence over addition, whichever side of a number it appeared on. Thus 3 + 4 × 5 = 5 × 4 + 3 = 23.
   a. Algebraic K-theory
   b. Identity element
   c. Isomorphism class
   d. Order of operations

17. _____ involves reducing the number of significant digits in a number. The result of _____ is a 'shorter' number having fewer non-zero digits yet similar in magnitude. The result is less precise but easier to use.
   a. Hyper operator
   b. Rounding
   c. Shabakh
   d. Sudan function

18. _____ is the calculated approximation of a result which is usable even if input data may be incomplete or uncertain.

In statistics, see _____ theory, estimator.

In mathematics, approximation or _____ typically means finding upper or lower bounds of a quantity that cannot readily be computed precisely and is also an educated guess .

a. U-statistic
b. Estimator
c. Estimation theory
d. Estimation

Chapter 4. DECIMAL NOTATION

1. In a positional numeral system, the decimal separator is a symbol used to mark the boundary between the integral and the fractional parts of a decimal numeral. When used in context of Arabic numerals, terms implying the symbol used are _____ and decimal comma.

   The decimal separator is mathematically a radix point.

   a. Fibonacci coding
   b. Tetradecimal
   c. Hexadecimal
   d. Decimal point

2. _____ is a numeral system in which each position is related to the next by a constant multiplier, a common ratio, called the base or radix of that numeral system.
   a. Place value
   b. Negative base
   c. NegaFibonacci coding
   d. Cyrillic numerals

3. In mathematics, a _____ is a number which can be expressed as a ratio of two integers. Non-integer _____s are usually written as the vulgar fraction $\frac{a}{b}$, where b is not zero. a is called the numerator, and b the denominator.
   a. Pre-algebra
   b. Minkowski distance
   c. Rational number
   d. Tally marks

4. In mathematics the concept of a _____ generalizes notions such as 'length', 'area', and 'volume'. Informally, given some base set, a '_____' is any consistent assignment of 'sizes' to the subsets of the base set. Depending on the application, the 'size' of a subset may be interpreted as its physical size, the amount of something that lies within the subset, or the probability that some random process will yield a result within the subset.
   a. Lattice
   b. Congruent
   c. Measure
   d. Cusp

Chapter 4. DECIMAL NOTATION

5. In mathematics, an _____ in the sense of ring theory is a subring $\mathcal{O}$ of a ring R that satisfies the conditions

   1. R is a ring which is a finite-dimensional algebra over the rational number field $\mathbb{Q}$
   2. $\mathcal{O}$ spans R over $\mathbb{Q}$, so that $\mathbb{Q}\mathcal{O} = R$, and
   3. $\mathcal{O}$ is a lattice in R.

The third condition can be stated more accurately, in terms of the extension of scalars of R to the real numbers, embedding R in a real vector space. In less formal terms, additively $\mathcal{O}$ should be a free abelian group generated by a basis for R over $\mathbb{Q}$.

The leading example is the case where R is a number field K and $\mathcal{O}$ is its ring of integers. In algebraic number theory there are examples for any K other than the rational field of proper subrings of the ring of integers that are also _____s.

- a. Order
- b. Efficiency
- c. Annihilator
- d. Algebraic

6. _____ involves reducing the number of significant digits in a number. The result of _____ is a 'shorter' number having fewer non-zero digits yet similar in magnitude. The result is less precise but easier to use.
- a. Rounding
- b. Shabakh
- c. Sudan function
- d. Hyper operator

7. An _____ is a number which is involved in addition. A number being added is considered to be an _____.
- a. A chemical equation
- b. A posteriori
- c. A Mathematical Theory of Communication
- d. Addend

8. In mathematics, the _____ of a number n is the number that, when added to n, yields zero. The _____ of n is denoted −n. For example, 7 is −7, because 7 + (−7) = 0, and the _____ of −0.3 is 0.3, because −0.3 + 0.3 = 0.

Chapter 4. DECIMAL NOTATION

a. Arity
b. Algebraic structure
c. Additive inverse
d. Associativity

9. A _____ is a device for performing mathematical calculations, distinguished from a computer by having a limited problem solving ability and an interface optimized for interactive calculation rather than programming. _____s can be hardware or software, and mechanical or electronic, and are often built into devices such as PDAs or mobile phones.

Modern electronic _____s are generally small, digital, and usually inexpensive.

a. 120-cell
b. 1-center problem
c. 2-3 heap
d. Calculator

10. In mathematics, a _____ can mean either an element of the set {1, 2, 3, ...} (i.e the positive integers) or an element of the set {0, 1, 2, 3, ...} (i.e. the non-negative integers).
a. FISH
b. Whole number
c. Bounded
d. Degrees of freedom

11. In the mathematical discipline of graph theory, a graph labeling is the assignment of labels, traditionally represented with integers, to the edges or vertices of a graph.

Formally, given a graph G: = with V being the set of vertices and E being the set of edges, a vertex labeling is a function from some subset of the integers to the verticies of the graph. A graph with such function defined is called a vertex-_____.

a. 2-3 heap
b. 1-center problem
c. 120-cell
d. Labeled graph

12. _____ is the mathematical operation of scaling one number by another. It is one of the four basic operations in elementary arithmetic.

_____ is defined for whole numbers in terms of repeated addition; for example, 4 multiplied by 3 can be calculated by adding 3 copies of 4 together:

$$4 + 4 + 4 = 12.$$

_____ of rational numbers and real numbers is defined by systematic generalization of this basic idea.

   a. Least common multiple
   b. Highest common factor
   c. The number 0 is even.
   d. Multiplication

13. In abstract algebra, a field extension L /K is called _____ if every element of L is _____ over K. Field extensions which are not _____.

For example, the field extension R/Q, that is the field of real numbers as an extension of the field of rational numbers, is transcendental, while the field extensions C/R and Q

   a. Identity
   b. Algebraic
   c. Ideal
   d. Echo

14. In mathematics and physics, there are a _____ number of topics named in honor of Leonhard Euler . As well, many of these topics include their own unique function, equation, formula, identity, number, or other mathematical entity. Unfortunately however, many of these entities have been given simple names like Euler's function, Euler's equation, and Euler's formula, which are further confused by variations of the 'Euler'-prefix Overall though, Euler's work touched upon so many fields that he is often the earliest written reference on a given matter.
   a. List of mathematical knots and links
   b. List of trigonometry topics
   c. List of integrals of logarithmic functions
   d. Large

15. In algebra and computer programming, when a number or expression is both preceded and followed by a binary operation, a rule is required for which operation should be applied first; this rule is known as an _____ . From the earliest use of mathematical notation, multiplication took precedence over addition, whichever side of a number it appeared on. Thus 3 + 4 × 5 = 5 × 4 + 3 = 23.

Chapter 4. DECIMAL NOTATION

a. Algebraic K-theory
b. Isomorphism class
c. Identity element
d. Order of operations

16. In mathematics, an _____, or central tendency of a data set refers to a measure of the 'middle' or 'expected' value of the data set. There are many different descriptive statistics that can be chosen as a measurement of the central tendency of the data items.

An _____ is a single value that is meant to typify a list of values.

a. A Mathematical Theory of Communication
b. A chemical equation
c. A posteriori
d. Average

17. A _____ is a deliberate process for transforming one or more inputs into one or more results, with variable change.

The term is used in a variety of senses, from the very definite arithmetical using an algorithm to the vague heuristics of calculating a strategy in a competition or calculating the chance of a successful relationship between two people.

Multiplying 7 by 8 is a simple algorithmic _____.

a. Mathematics Subject Classification
b. Mathematical object
c. Mathematical maturity
d. Calculation

18. In mathematics, a _____ is the end result of a division problem. It can also be expressed as the number of times the divisor divides into the dividend.

a. Notation
b. Limiting
c. Marginal cost
d. Quotient

Chapter 5. RATIO AND PROPORTION

1. _____ is a special mathematical relationship between two quantities. Two quantities are called proportional if they vary in such a way that one of the quantities is a constant multiple of the other, or equivalently if they have a constant ratio.
   a. Discontinuity
   b. Depth
   c. Compression
   d. Proportionality

2. In mathematics, two quantities are called _____ if they vary in such a way that one of the quantities is a constant multiple of the other, or equivalently if they have a constant ratio.
   a. 1-center problem
   b. 120-cell
   c. 2-3 heap
   d. Proportional

3. A _____ is a software program that facilitates symbolic mathematics. The core functionality of a CAS is manipulation of mathematical expressions in symbolic form.

Chapter 5. RATIO AND PROPORTION

The symbolic manipulations supported typically include

- simplification to the smallest possible expression or some standard form, including automatic simplification with assumptions and simplification with constraints
- substitution of symbolic, functors or numeric values for expressions
- change of form of expressions: expanding products and powers, partial and full factorization, rewriting as partial fractions, constraint satisfaction, rewriting trigonometric functions as exponentials, etc.
- partial and total differentiation
- symbolic constrained and unconstrained global optimization
- solution of linear and some non-linear equations over various domains
- solution of some differential and difference equations
- taking some limits
- some indefinite and definite integration, including multidimensional integrals
- integral transforms
- arbitrary-precision numeric operations
- Series operations such as expansion, summation and products
- matrix operations including products, inverses, etc.
- display of mathematical expressions in two-dimensional mathematical form, often using typesetting systems similar to TeX
- add-ons for use in applied mathematics such as physics packages for physical computation
- plotting graphs and parametric plots of functions in two and three dimensions, and animating them
- APIs for linking it on an external program such as a database, or using in a programming language to use the _____
- drawing charts and diagrams
- string manipulation such as matching and searching
- statistical computation
- Theorem proving and verification
- graphic production and editing such as CGI and signal processing as image processing
- sound synthesis

Many also include a programming language, allowing users to implement their own algorithms.

Some _____s focus on a specific area of application; these are typically developed in academia and are free.

a. 120-cell
b. Computer algebra system
c. 1-center problem
d. 2-3 heap

4. _____ is the mathematical operation of scaling one number by another. It is one of the four basic operations in elementary arithmetic.

Chapter 5. RATIO AND PROPORTION

_____ is defined for whole numbers in terms of repeated addition; for example, 4 multiplied by 3 can be calculated by adding 3 copies of 4 together:

$$4 + 4 + 4 = 12.$$

_____ of rational numbers and real numbers is defined by systematic generalization of this basic idea.

a. Multiplication
b. The number 0 is even.
c. Highest common factor
d. Least common multiple

5. A _____ is a device for performing mathematical calculations, distinguished from a computer by having a limited problem solving ability and an interface optimized for interactive calculation rather than programming. _____s can be hardware or software, and mechanical or electronic, and are often built into devices such as PDAs or mobile phones.

Modern electronic _____s are generally small, digital, and usually inexpensive.

a. 1-center problem
b. 120-cell
c. Calculator
d. 2-3 heap

6. In mathematics, a _____ can mean either an element of the set {1, 2, 3, ...} (i.e the positive integers) or an element of the set {0, 1, 2, 3, ...} (i.e. the non-negative integers).
a. Degrees of freedom
b. Bounded
c. Whole number
d. FISH

7. _____ involves reducing the number of significant digits in a number. The result of _____ is a 'shorter' number having fewer non-zero digits yet similar in magnitude. The result is less precise but easier to use.
a. Hyper operator
b. Rounding
c. Shabakh
d. Sudan function

Chapter 5. RATIO AND PROPORTION

8. In mathematics, an _____, or central tendency of a data set refers to a measure of the 'middle' or 'expected' value of the data set. There are many different descriptive statistics that can be chosen as a measurement of the central tendency of the data items.

An _____ is a single value that is meant to typify a list of values.

   a. A Mathematical Theory of Communication
   b. A posteriori
   c. A chemical equation
   d. Average

9. In linear algebra, two n-by-n matrices A and B over the field K are called _____ if there exists an invertible n-by-n matrix P over K such that

$$P^{-1}AP = B.$$

One of the meanings of the term similarity transformation is such a transformation of a matrix A into a matrix B.

Similarity is an equivalence relation on the space of square matrices.

_____ matrices share many properties:

- rank
- determinant
- trace
- eigenvalues
- characteristic polynomial
- minimal polynomial
- elementary divisors

There are two reasons for these facts:

- two _____ matrices can be thought of as describing the same linear map, but with respect to different bases
- the map $X \mapsto P^{-1}XP$ is an automorphism of the associative algebra of all n-by-n matrices, as the one-object case of the above category of all matrices.

Because of this, for a given matrix A, one is interested in finding a simple 'normal form' B which is _____ to A -- the study of A then reduces to the study of the simpler matrix B.

Chapter 5. RATIO AND PROPORTION

    a. Similar
    b. Dense
    c. Blinding
    d. Coherence

10.

_____ is a Unicode block of 96 symbols at hex codepoint range 25A0-25FF. This range contains various _____.

Only two font sets--Code2000 and the DejaVu family--include coverage for each of the glyphs in the _____ range.

    a. Geometric shapes
    b. 2-3 heap
    c. 1-center problem
    d. 120-cell

11. The _____ of an object located in some space refers to the part of space occupied by the object as determined by its external boundary -- abstracting from other aspects the object may have such as its colour, content as well as from the object's position and orientation in space, and its size.

According to famous mathematician and statistician David George Kendall, _____ may be defined as

Simple two-dimensional _____s can be described by basic geometry such as points, line, curves, plane, and so on. _____s that occur in the physical world are often quite complex; they may be arbitrarily curved as studied by differential geometry as for plants or coastlines.)

    a. Confocal
    b. Shape
    c. Spidron
    d. Parallel lines

12. A _____ is one of the basic shapes of geometry: a polygon with three corners or vertices and three sides or edges which are line segments. A _____ with vertices A, B, and C is denoted ABC.

In Euclidean geometry any three non-collinear points determine a unique _____ and a unique plane.

Chapter 5. RATIO AND PROPORTION

a. 1-center problem
b. Kepler triangle
c. Triangle
d. Fuhrmann circle

Chapter 6. PERCENT NOTATION

1. A _____ is a circular chart divided into sectors, illustrating relative magnitudes or frequences or percents. In a _____, the arc length of each sector, is proportional to the quantity it represents. Together, the sectors create a full disk.
    a. Pie chart
    b. 2-3 heap
    c. 120-cell
    d. 1-center problem

2. A _____ is a device for performing mathematical calculations, distinguished from a computer by having a limited problem solving ability and an interface optimized for interactive calculation rather than programming. _____s can be hardware or software, and mechanical or electronic, and are often built into devices such as PDAs or mobile phones.

    Modern electronic _____s are generally small, digital, and usually inexpensive.

    a. 120-cell
    b. 1-center problem
    c. 2-3 heap
    d. Calculator

3. In mathematics the concept of a _____ generalizes notions such as 'length', 'area', and 'volume'. Informally, given some base set, a '_____' is any consistent assignment of 'sizes' to the subsets of the base set. Depending on the application, the 'size' of a subset may be interpreted as its physical size, the amount of something that lies within the subset, or the probability that some random process will yield a result within the subset.
    a. Lattice
    b. Congruent
    c. Measure
    d. Cusp

4. In mathematics, a _____ can mean either an element of the set {1, 2, 3, ...} (i.e the positive integers) or an element of the set {0, 1, 2, 3, ...} (i.e. the non-negative integers).
    a. Degrees of freedom
    b. FISH
    c. Bounded
    d. Whole number

5. In the study of metric spaces in mathematics, there are various notions of two metrics on the same underlying space being 'the same', or _____.

In the following, M will denote a non-empty set and d_1 and d_2 will denote two metrics on M.

Chapter 6. PERCENT NOTATION

The two metrics d_1 and d_2 are said to be topologically _____ if they generate the same topology on M.

a. A chemical equation
b. Equivalent
c. A posteriori
d. A Mathematical Theory of Communication

6. _____ is a general term for any type of information processing. This includes phenomena ranging from human thinking to calculations with a more narrow meaning. _____ is a process following a well-defined model that is understood and can be expressed in an algorithm, protocol, network topology, etc.
   a. 120-cell
   b. 1-center problem
   c. 2-3 heap
   d. Computation

7. _____ is a special mathematical relationship between two quantities. Two quantities are called proportional if they vary in such a way that one of the quantities is a constant multiple of the other, or equivalently if they have a constant ratio.
   a. Depth
   b. Discontinuity
   c. Proportionality
   d. Compression

8. _____ is a fee, paid on borrowed capital. Assets lent include money, shares, consumer goods through hire purchase, major assets such as aircraft, and even entire factories in finance lease arrangements. The _____ is calculated upon the value of the assets in the same manner as upon money.
   a. A Mathematical Theory of Communication
   b. Interest sensitivity gap
   c. Interest expense
   d. Interest

9. In abstract algebra, a module S over a ring R is called _____ or irreducible if it is not the zero module 0 and if its only submodules are 0 and S. Understanding the _____ modules over a ring is usually helpful because these modules form the 'building blocks' of all other modules in a certain sense.

Abelian groups are the same as Z-modules.

Chapter 6. PERCENT NOTATION

   a. Derivation
   b. Simple
   c. Harmonic series
   d. Basis

10. _____ is the concept of adding accumulated interest back to the principal, so that interest is earned on interest from that moment on. The act of declaring interest to be principal is called compounding. A loan, for example, may have its interest compounded every month: in this case, a loan with $100 principal and 1% interest per month would have a balance of $101 at the end of the first month.
   a. Compound interest
   b. Retained interest
   c. Net interest margin securities
   d. Net interest margin

11. The terms _____, nominal APR, and effective APR describe the interest rate for a whole year, rather than just a monthly fee/rate, as applied on a loan, mortgage, credit card, etc. Those terms have formal, legal definitions in some countries or legal jurisdictions, but in general:

   - The nominal APR is the simple-interest rate.
   - The effective APR is the fee+compound interest rate.

The nominal APR is calculated as: the rate, for a payment period, multiplied by the number of payment periods in a year. However, the exact legal definition of 'effective APR' can vary greatly in each jurisdiction, depending on the type of fees included, such as participation fees, loan origination fees, monthly service charges, or late fees. The effective APR has been called the 'mathematically-true' interest rate for each year. The computation for the effective APR, as the fee+compound interest rate, can also vary depending on whether the up-front fees, such as origination or participation fees, are added to the entire amount, or treated as a short-term loan due in the first payment.

   a. A chemical equation
   b. A Mathematical Theory of Communication
   c. A posteriori
   d. Annual percentage rate

12. In mathematics, a _____ is a way of expressing a number as a fraction of 100. It is often denoted using the percent sign, '%'. For example, 45% is equal to 45 / 100, or 0.45.

Chapter 6. PERCENT NOTATION

a. Subtrahend
b. Lowest common denominator
c. Percentage
d. Least common multiple

13. _____ or amortisation is the process of decreasing an amount over a period of time. The word comes from Middle English amortisen to kill, alienate in mortmain, from Anglo-French amorteser, alteration of amortir, from Vulgar Latin admortire to kill, from Latin ad- + mort-, mors death. Particular instances of the term include:

- _____, the allocation of a lump sum amount to different time periods, particularly for loans and other forms of finance, including related interest or other finance charges.
    - _____ schedule, a table detailing each periodic payment on a loan, as generated by an _____ calculator.
    - Negative _____, an _____ schedule where the loan amount actually increases through not paying the full interest
- Amortized analysis, analyzing the execution cost of algorithms over a sequence of operations.
- _____ of capital expenditures of certain assets under accounting rules, particularly intangible assets, in a manner analogous to depreciation.
- _____

_____ is also used in the context of zoning regulations and describes the time in which a property owner has to relocate when the property's use constitutes a preexisting nonconforming use under zoning regulations.

- Depreciation

a. Identity
b. ISAAC
c. Origin
d. Amortization

Chapter 7. DATA, GRAPHS, AND STATISTICS

1. _____ is a process of gathering, modeling, and transforming data with the goal of highlighting useful information, suggesting conclusions, and supporting decision making. _____ has multiple facets and approaches, encompassing diverse techniques under a variety of names, in different business, science, and social science domains.

   Data mining is a particular _____ technique that focuses on modeling and knowledge discovery for predictive rather than purely descriptive purposes.

   a. Data analysis
   b. Subgroup analysis
   c. Power transform
   d. Double mass analysis

2. _____ or pictograph is a symbol representing a concept, object, activity, place or event by illustration. Pictography is a form of writing in which ideas are transmitted through drawing. It is a basis of cuneiform and, to some extent, hieroglyphic writing, which uses drawings also as phonetic letters or determinative rhymes.
   a. Sparkline
   b. Pictographs
   c. Treemapping
   d. Pictogram

3. _____ are symbols representing a concept, object, activity, place or event by illustration.
   a. Sparkline
   b. Pictogram
   c. Treemapping
   d. Pictographs

4. In mathematics, one method of defining a group is by a _____. One specifies a set S of generators so that every element of the group can be written as a product of some of these generators, and a set R of relations among those generators. We then say G has _____

   $$\langle S \mid R \rangle.$$

   Informally, G has the above _____ if it is the 'freest group' generated by S subject only to the relations R.

   a. 1-center problem
   b. Tietze transformations
   c. 120-cell
   d. Presentation

Chapter 7. DATA, GRAPHS, AND STATISTICS

5. A bar chart or _____ is a chart with rectangular bars with lengths proportional to the values that they represent. Bar charts are used for comparing two or more values. The bars can be horizontally or vertically oriented.
   a. 1-center problem
   b. 2-3 heap
   c. 120-cell
   d. Bar graph

6. The term _____ or centre is used in various contexts in abstract algebra to denote the set of all those elements that commute with all other elements. More specifically:

   - The _____ of a group G consists of all those elements x in G such that xg = gx for all g in G. This is a normal subgroup of G.
   - The _____ of a ring R is the subset of R consisting of all those elements x of R such that xr = rx for all r in R. The _____ is a commutative subring of R, so R is an algebra over its _____.
   - The _____ of an algebra A consists of all those elements x of A such that xa = ax for all a in A. See also: central simple algebra.
   - The _____ of a Lie algebra L consists of all those elements x in L such that [x,a] = 0 for all a in L. This is an ideal of the Lie algebra L.
   - The _____ of a monoidal category C consists of pairs *a natural isomorphism satisfying certain axioms*.

   a. Center
   b. Disk
   c. Block size
   d. Brute Force

7. In mathematics, an average, or _____ of a data set refers to a measure of the 'middle' or 'expected' value of the data set. There are many different descriptive statistics that can be chosen as a measurement of the _____ of the data items.

   An average is a single value that is meant to typify a list of values.

   a. Central tendency
   b. Trimean
   c. Mean reciprocal rank
   d. Quartile

8. In a graph theory, the _____ L

Chapter 7. DATA, GRAPHS, AND STATISTICS

One of the earliest and most important theorems about _____s is due to Hassler Whitney, who proved that with one exceptional case the structure of G can be recovered completely from its _____.

a. Line graph
b. Vertex-transitive graph
c. Bivariegated graph
d. Sparse graph

9. In mathematics the concept of a _____ generalizes notions such as 'length', 'area', and 'volume'. Informally, given some base set, a '_____' is any consistent assignment of 'sizes' to the subsets of the base set. Depending on the application, the 'size' of a subset may be interpreted as its physical size, the amount of something that lies within the subset, or the probability that some random process will yield a result within the subset.

a. Congruent
b. Cusp
c. Lattice
d. Measure

10. A _____ is the result of applying a function to a set of data.

More formally, statistical theory defines a _____ as a function of a sample where the function itself is independent of the sample's distribution: the term is used both for the function and for the value of the function on a given sample.

A _____ is distinct from an unknown statistical parameter, which is not computable from a sample.

a. Parameter space
b. Loss function
c. Spatial dependence
d. Statistic

11. In mathematics and statistics, the _____ of a list of numbers is the sum of all of the list divided by the number of items in the list. If the list is a statistical population, then the mean of that population is called a population mean. If the list is a statistical sample, we call the resulting statistic a sample mean.

a. Interval estimation
b. Unsolved problems in statistics
c. Analysis of variance
d. Arithmetic mean

Chapter 7. DATA, GRAPHS, AND STATISTICS

12. In mathematics, an _____, or central tendency of a data set refers to a measure of the 'middle' or 'expected' value of the data set. There are many different descriptive statistics that can be chosen as a measurement of the central tendency of the data items.

An _____ is a single value that is meant to typify a list of values.

a. A posteriori
b. A chemical equation
c. A Mathematical Theory of Communication
d. Average

13. In statistics, _____ has two related meanings:

- the arithmetic _____.
- the expected value of a random variable, which is also called the population _____.

It is sometimes stated that the '_____' _____s average. This is incorrect if '_____' is taken in the specific sense of 'arithmetic _____' as there are different types of averages: the _____, median, and mode. For instance, average house prices almost always use the median value for the average.

For a real-valued random variable X, the _____ is the expectation of X.

a. Mean
b. Probability
c. Statistical population
d. Proportional hazards model

14. In the physical sciences, _____ is a measurement of the gravitational force acting on an object. Near the surface of the Earth, the acceleration due to gravity is approximately constant; this means that an object's _____ is roughly proportional to its mass.

In commerce and in many other applications, _____ means the same as mass as that term is used in physics.

a. 1-center problem
b. 120-cell
c. 2-3 heap
d. Weight

Chapter 7. DATA, GRAPHS, AND STATISTICS

15. A _____ is a device for performing mathematical calculations, distinguished from a computer by having a limited problem solving ability and an interface optimized for interactive calculation rather than programming. _____s can be hardware or software, and mechanical or electronic, and are often built into devices such as PDAs or mobile phones.

Modern electronic _____s are generally small, digital, and usually inexpensive.

   a. Calculator
   b. 2-3 heap
   c. 120-cell
   d. 1-center problem

16. In mathematics, a _____ can mean either an element of the set {1, 2, 3, ...} (i.e the positive integers) or an element of the set {0, 1, 2, 3, ...} (i.e. the non-negative integers).
   a. Degrees of freedom
   b. FISH
   c. Bounded
   d. Whole number

17. In geometry, a _____ of a triangle is a line segment joining a vertex to the midpoint of the opposing side. Every triangle has exactly three _____s; one running from each vertex to the opposite side.

The three _____s are concurrent at a point known as the triangle's centroid, or center of mass of the triangle.

   a. Correlation
   b. Statistical significance
   c. Percentile rank
   d. Median

18. In statistics, the _____ is the value that occurs the most frequently in a data set or a probability distribution. In some fields, notably education, sample data are often called scores, and the sample _____ is known as the modal score.

Like the statistical mean and the median, the _____ is a way of capturing important information about a random variable or a population in a single quantity.

a. Function
b. Deltoid
c. Field
d. Mode

19. A _____ is a simple shape of Euclidean geometry consisting of those points in a plane which are at a constant distance, called the radius, from a fixed point, called the center. A _____ with center A is sometimes denoted by the symbol A.

A chord of a _____ is a line segment whose two endpoints lie on the _____.

a. Malfatti circles
b. Circular segment
c. Circumcircle
d. Circle

20. In graph theory, a _____ is a graph whose vertices can be associated with chords of a circle such that two vertices are adjacent if and only if the corresponding chords in the circle intersect.

Spinrad (1994) gives an $O(n^2)$-time recognition algorithm for _____s that also computes a circle model of the input graph if it is a _____.

A number of other problems that are NP-complete on general graphs have polynomial time algorithms when restricted to _____s.

a. Sparse graph
b. Vertex-transitive graph
c. Planar graph
d. Circle graph

21. A _____ is a circular chart divided into sectors, illustrating relative magnitudes or frequences or percents. In a _____, the arc length of each sector, is proportional to the quantity it represents. Together, the sectors create a full disk.
a. 1-center problem
b. 120-cell
c. 2-3 heap
d. Pie chart

Chapter 8. MEASUREMENT

1. _____ is a quantity expressing the two-dimensional size of a defined part of a surface, typically a region bounded by a closed curve. The term surface _____ refers to the total _____ of the exposed surface of a 3-dimensional solid, such as the sum of the _____s of the exposed sides of a polyhedron. _____ is an important invariant in the differential geometry of surfaces.

   a. Area
   b. A chemical equation
   c. A Mathematical Theory of Communication
   d. A posteriori

2. In mathematics the concept of a _____ generalizes notions such as 'length', 'area', and 'volume'. Informally, given some base set, a '_____' is any consistent assignment of 'sizes' to the subsets of the base set. Depending on the application, the 'size' of a subset may be interpreted as its physical size, the amount of something that lies within the subset, or the probability that some random process will yield a result within the subset.

   a. Measure
   b. Lattice
   c. Cusp
   d. Congruent

3. _____ is the mathematical operation of scaling one number by another. It is one of the four basic operations in elementary arithmetic.

   _____ is defined for whole numbers in terms of repeated addition; for example, 4 multiplied by 3 can be calculated by adding 3 copies of 4 together:

   $$4 + 4 + 4 = 12.$$

   _____ of rational numbers and real numbers is defined by systematic generalization of this basic idea.

   a. Highest common factor
   b. The number 0 is even.
   c. Least common multiple
   d. Multiplication

4. In abstract algebra, a field extension L /K is called _____ if every element of L is _____ over K. Field extensions which are not _____.

For example, the field extension R/Q, that is the field of real numbers as an extension of the field of rational numbers, is transcendental, while the field extensions C/R and Q

Chapter 8. MEASUREMENT

a. Ideal
b. Echo
c. Algebraic
d. Identity

5. A _____ is any one of many units of measure used by various ancient peoples and is among the first recorded units of length.

The _____ is based on measuring by comparing - especially cords and textiles, but also for timbers and stones - to one's forearm length. The Egyptian hieroglyph for the unit shows this symbol.

a. 120-cell
b. 1-center problem
c. 2-3 heap
d. Cubit

6. The _____ is a decimalised system of measurement. It exists in several variations, with different choices of base units, though the choice of base units does not affect its day-to-day use. Over the last two centuries, different variants have been considered the _____.

a. George Dantzig
b. 1-center problem
c. Nonlinear system
d. Metric system

7. In the physical sciences, _____ is a measurement of the gravitational force acting on an object. Near the surface of the Earth, the acceleration due to gravity is approximately constant; this means that an object's _____ is roughly proportional to its mass.

In commerce and in many other applications, _____ means the same as mass as that term is used in physics.

a. Weight
b. 1-center problem
c. 2-3 heap
d. 120-cell

8. A _____ is a software program that facilitates symbolic mathematics. The core functionality of a CAS is manipulation of mathematical expressions in symbolic form.

Chapter 8. MEASUREMENT

The symbolic manipulations supported typically include

- simplification to the smallest possible expression or some standard form, including automatic simplification with assumptions and simplification with constraints
- substitution of symbolic, functors or numeric values for expressions
- change of form of expressions: expanding products and powers, partial and full factorization, rewriting as partial fractions, constraint satisfaction, rewriting trigonometric functions as exponentials, etc.
- partial and total differentiation
- symbolic constrained and unconstrained global optimization
- solution of linear and some non-linear equations over various domains
- solution of some differential and difference equations
- taking some limits
- some indefinite and definite integration, including multidimensional integrals
- integral transforms
- arbitrary-precision numeric operations
- Series operations such as expansion, summation and products
- matrix operations including products, inverses, etc.
- display of mathematical expressions in two-dimensional mathematical form, often using typesetting systems similar to TeX
- add-ons for use in applied mathematics such as physics packages for physical computation
- plotting graphs and parametric plots of functions in two and three dimensions, and animating them
- APIs for linking it on an external program such as a database, or using in a programming language to use the _____
- drawing charts and diagrams
- string manipulation such as matching and searching
- statistical computation
- Theorem proving and verification
- graphic production and editing such as CGI and signal processing as image processing
- sound synthesis

Many also include a programming language, allowing users to implement their own algorithms.

Some _____s focus on a specific area of application; these are typically developed in academia and are free.

a. 1-center problem
b. 2-3 heap
c. 120-cell
d. Computer algebra system

9. In computational complexity theory, an algorithm is said to take _____ if the asymptotic upper bound for the time it requires is proportional to the size of the input, which is usually denoted n.

Chapter 8. MEASUREMENT

Informally spoken, the running time increases linearly with the size of the input. For example, a procedure that adds up all elements of a list requires time proportional to the length of the list.

a. Time-constructible function
b. Truth table reduction
c. Linear time
d. Constructible function

10. _____ is a temperature scale that is named after the German physicist Daniel Gabriel _____, who proposed it in 1724.

In this scale, the freezing point of water is 32 degrees _____ and the boiling point 212 °F, placing the boiling and freezing points of water exactly 180 degrees apart. A degree on the _____ scale is 1/180th part of the interval between the ice point and the boiling point.

a. 120-cell
b. 2-3 heap
c. 1-center problem
d. Fahrenheit

11. A _____ is a device for performing mathematical calculations, distinguished from a computer by having a limited problem solving ability and an interface optimized for interactive calculation rather than programming. _____s can be hardware or software, and mechanical or electronic, and are often built into devices such as PDAs or mobile phones.

Modern electronic _____s are generally small, digital, and usually inexpensive.

a. 2-3 heap
b. Calculator
c. 1-center problem
d. 120-cell

12. In mathematics, a _____ can mean either an element of the set {1, 2, 3, ...} (i.e the positive integers) or an element of the set {0, 1, 2, 3, ...} (i.e. the non-negative integers).
a. FISH
b. Degrees of freedom
c. Bounded
d. Whole number

13. In computer science an _____ is a data structure consisting of a group of elements that are accessed by indexing. In most programming languages each element has the same data type and the _____ occupies a contiguous area of storage.

Most programming languages have a built-in _____ data type, although what is called an _____ in the language documentation is sometimes really an associative _____.

   a. A posteriori
   b. A Mathematical Theory of Communication
   c. A chemical equation
   d. Array

Chapter 9. GEOMETRY

1. The _____ is the length of the line that bounds an area In the special case where the area is circular, the _____ is known as the circumference.
   a. Concyclic
   b. Perimeter
   c. Reflection symmetry
   d. Multilateration

2. In geometry a _____ is traditionally a plane figure that is bounded by a closed path or circuit, composed of a finite sequence of straight line segments. These segments are called its edges or sides, and the points where two edges meet are the _____'s vertices or corners. The interior of the _____ is sometimes called its body.
   a. Polygonal curve
   b. Regular polygon
   c. Parallelogon
   d. Polygon

3. In geometry, a _____ is defined as a quadrilateral where all four of its angles are right angles.
   a. Polytope
   b. Rectangle
   c. Cantor-Dedekind axiom
   d. Point group in two dimensions

4. _____ is a quantity expressing the two-dimensional size of a defined part of a surface, typically a region bounded by a closed curve. The term surface _____ refers to the total _____ of the exposed surface of a 3-dimensional solid, such as the sum of the _____s of the exposed sides of a polyhedron. _____ is an important invariant in the differential geometry of surfaces.
   a. A Mathematical Theory of Communication
   b. Area
   c. A posteriori
   d. A chemical equation

5. In computer science an _____ is a data structure consisting of a group of elements that are accessed by indexing. In most programming languages each element has the same data type and the _____ occupies a contiguous area of storage.

Most programming languages have a built-in _____ data type, although what is called an _____ in the language documentation is sometimes really an associative _____.

Chapter 9. GEOMETRY

a. A Mathematical Theory of Communication
b. Array
c. A posteriori
d. A chemical equation

6. In mathematics and computer science, _____ (also base-16, hexa or base, of 16. It uses sixteen distinct symbols, most often the symbols 0-9 to represent values zero to nine, and A, B, C, D, E, F (or a through f) to represent values ten to fifteen.

Its primary use is as a human friendly representation of binary coded values, so it is often used in digital electronics and computer engineering.

a. Hexadecimal
b. Tetradecimal
c. Radix
d. Factoradic

7. _____ is the measurement of vertical distance, but has two meanings in common use. It can either indicate how 'tall' something is, or how 'high up' it is. For example one could say 'That is a tall building', or 'That airplane is high up in the sky'.
a. 1-center problem
b. 2-3 heap
c. 120-cell
d. Height

8. In geometry, a _____ is a quadrilateral with two sets of parallel sides. The opposite sides of a _____ are of equal length, and the opposite angles of a _____ are congruent. The three-dimensional counterpart of a _____ is a parallelepiped.
a. 120-cell
b. 1-center problem
c. 2-3 heap
d. Parallelogram

9. Scientific notation, also sometimes known as standard form or as _____, is a way of writing numbers that accommodates values too large or small to be conveniently written in standard decimal notation. Scientific notation has a number of useful properties and is often favored by scientists, mathematicians and engineers, who work with such numbers.

Chapter 9. GEOMETRY

In scientific notation, numbers are written in the form:

$$a \times 10^b$$

a. A Mathematical Theory of Communication
b. A posteriori
c. A chemical equation
d. Exponential notation

10. A _____ is one of the basic shapes of geometry: a polygon with three corners or vertices and three sides or edges which are line segments. A _____ with vertices A, B, and C is denoted ABC.

In Euclidean geometry any three non-collinear points determine a unique _____ and a unique plane.

a. Triangle
b. Kepler triangle
c. 1-center problem
d. Fuhrmann circle

11. A _____ or a trapezium is a quadrilateral that has at least one pair of parallel lines for sides.

Some authors define it as a quadrilateral having exactly one pair of parallel sides, so as to exclude parallelograms, which otherwise would be regarded as a special type of _____, but most mathematicians use the inclusive definition.

In North America, the term trapezium is used to refer to a quadrilateral with no parallel sides.

a. Trapezium
b. Lozenge
c. Rhomboid
d. Trapezoid

12. A _____ is a simple shape of Euclidean geometry consisting of those points in a plane which are at a constant distance, called the radius, from a fixed point, called the center. A _____ with center A is sometimes denoted by the symbol A.

A chord of a _____ is a line segment whose two endpoints lie on the _____.

a. Circular segment
b. Malfatti circles
c. Circumcircle
d. Circle

13. In classical geometry, a _____ of a circle or sphere is any line segment from its center to its boundary. By extension, the _____ of a circle or sphere is the length of any such segment. The _____ is half the diameter. In science and engineering the term _____ of curvature is commonly used as a synonym for _____.

a. Birational geometry
b. Non-Euclidean geometry
c. Radius
d. Duoprism

14. The _____ is the distance around a closed curve. _____ is a kind of perimeter.

The _____ of a circle is the length around it.

a. Flatness
b. Circumference
c. Compactness measure of a shape
d. Brascamp-Lieb inequality

15. The _____ of any solid, plasma, vacuum or theoretical object is how much three-dimensional space it occupies, often quantified numerically. One-dimensional figures and two-dimensional shapes are assigned zero _____ in the three-dimensional space. _____ is presented as ml or cm^3.

_____s of straight-edged and circular shapes are calculated using arithmetic formulae.

a. Stress-energy tensor
b. Volume
c. Thermodynamic limit
d. Cauchy momentum equation

16. In mathematics, the _____s are analogs of the ordinary trigonometric functions. The basic _____s are the hyperbolic sine 'sinh', and the hyperbolic cosine 'cosh', from which are derived the hyperbolic tangent 'tanh', etc., in analogy to the derived trigonometric functions. The inverse _____ are the area hyperbolic sine 'arsinh' (also called 'asinh', or sometimes by the misnomer of 'arcsinh') and so on.

a. Rectangular function
b. Heaviside step function
c. Square root
d. Hyperbolic function

17. A _____ is a three-dimensional geometric shape that tapers smoothly from a flat, round base to a point called the apex or vertex. More precisely, it is the solid figure bounded by a plane base and the surface formed by the locus of all straight line segments joining the apex to the perimeter of the base. The term '_____' sometimes refers just to the surface of this solid figure, or just to the lateral surface.
   a. Characteristic
   b. Gravity waves
   c. Cone
   d. Blocking

18. In common usage, a cylinder is taken to mean a finite section of a right _____ with its ends closed to form two circular surfaces, as in the figure (right.) If the cylinder has a radius r and length (height) h, then its volume is given by

$$V = \pi r^2 h$$

and its surface area is:

- the area of the top (πr^2) +
- the area of the bottom (πr^2) +
- the area of the side $(2\pi rh)$.

Therefore without the top or bottom (lateral area), the surface area is

$$A = 2\pi rh.$$

With the top and bottom, the surface area is

$$A = 2\pi r^2 + 2\pi rh = 2\pi r(r+h).$$

For a given volume, the cylinder with the smallest surface area has h = 2r. For a given surface area, the cylinder with the largest volume has h = 2r, i.e. the cylinder fits in a cube (height = diameter.)

Cylindric sections are the intersections of cylinders with planes.

a. 120-cell
b. 1-center problem
c. 2-3 heap
d. Circular cylinder

19. In mathematics, a _____ is a quadric surface, with the following equation in Cartesian coordinates: $(x/a)^2 + (y/b)^2 = 1$.

a. Derivative algebra
b. Free
c. Discontinuity
d. Cylinder

20. A _____ is a symmetrical geometrical object. In non-mathematical usage, the term is used to refer either to a round ball or to its two-dimensional surface. In mathematics, a _____ is the set of all points in three-dimensional space which are at distance r from a fixed point of that space, where r is a positive real number called the radius of the _____.

a. Differentiable manifold
b. Differential geometry of curves
c. Lie derivative
d. Sphere

21. A _____ is a device for performing mathematical calculations, distinguished from a computer by having a limited problem solving ability and an interface optimized for interactive calculation rather than programming. _____s can be hardware or software, and mechanical or electronic, and are often built into devices such as PDAs or mobile phones.

Modern electronic _____s are generally small, digital, and usually inexpensive.

a. 120-cell
b. 1-center problem
c. 2-3 heap
d. Calculator

22. In mathematics, a _____ can mean either an element of the set {1, 2, 3, ...} (i.e the positive integers) or an element of the set {0, 1, 2, 3, ...} (i.e. the non-negative integers).

a. Bounded
b. FISH
c. Degrees of freedom
d. Whole number

23. In geometry and trigonometry, an _____ is the figure formed by two rays sharing a common endpoint, called the vertex of the _____. The magnitude of the _____ is the 'amount of rotation' that separates the two rays, and can be measured by considering the length of circular arc swept out when one ray is rotated about the vertex to coincide with the other. Where there is no possibility of confusion, the term '_____' is used interchangeably for both the geometric configuration itself and for its angular magnitude.
   a. A Mathematical Theory of Communication
   b. A chemical equation
   c. A posteriori
   d. Angle

24. In mathematics the concept of a _____ generalizes notions such as 'length', 'area', and 'volume'. Informally, given some base set, a '_____' is any consistent assignment of 'sizes' to the subsets of the base set. Depending on the application, the 'size' of a subset may be interpreted as its physical size, the amount of something that lies within the subset, or the probability that some random process will yield a result within the subset.
   a. Lattice
   b. Cusp
   c. Congruent
   d. Measure

25. _____ is the mathematical operation of scaling one number by another. It is one of the four basic operations in elementary arithmetic.

_____ is defined for whole numbers in terms of repeated addition; for example, 4 multiplied by 3 can be calculated by adding 3 copies of 4 together:

$$4 + 4 + 4 = 12.$$

_____ of rational numbers and real numbers is defined by systematic generalization of this basic idea.

   a. Highest common factor
   b. Multiplication
   c. Least common multiple
   d. The number 0 is even.

Chapter 9. GEOMETRY

26. In mathematics, the multiplicative inverse of a number x, denoted 1/x or x $^{-1}$, is the number which, when multiplied by x, yields 1. The multiplicative inverse of x is also called the _____ of x.
    a. 120-cell
    b. 2-3 heap
    c. 1-center problem
    d. Reciprocal

27. In geometry, a _____ is a special kind of point, usually a corner of a polygon, polyhedron, or higher dimensional polytope. In the geometry of curves a _____ is a point of where the first derivative of curvature is zero. In graph theory, a _____ is the fundamental unit out of which graphs are formed
    a. Duality
    b. Dini
    c. Crib
    d. Vertex

28. An angle smaller than a right angle is called an _____ (less than 90 degrees).
    a. Euclidean geometry
    b. Integral geometry
    c. Ultraparallel theorem
    d. Acute angle

29. In geometry and trigonometry, a _____ is defined as an angle between two straight intersecting lines of ninety degrees, or one-quarter of a circle.
    a. Trigonometric functions
    b. Trigonometry
    c. Sine integral
    d. Right angle

30. An angle equal to two right angles is called a _____ (equal to 180 degrees).
    a. Loomis-Whitney inequality
    b. Householder transformation
    c. Theorem
    d. Straight angle

31. A pair of angles are complementary if the sum of their measures add up to 90 degrees.

Chapter 9. GEOMETRY

If the two _____ are adjacent (i.e. have a common vertex and share a side, but do not have any interior points in common) their non-shared sides form a right angle.

In Euclidean geometry, the two acute angles in a right triangle are complementary, because there are 180>° in a triangle and 90>° have been accounted for by the right angle.

   a. Complementary angles
   b. Hypotenuse
   c. Conway polyhedron notation
   d. Quincunx

32.   A pair of angles is _____ if their measurements add up to 180 degrees. If the two _____ angles are adjacent their non-shared sides form a straight line. The supplement of 135 would be 45.
   a. FISH
   b. Dense
   c. Cylinder
   d. Supplementary

33.   In geometry, an _____ is a triangle in which all three sides have equal lengths. In traditional or Euclidean geometry, _____s are also equiangular; that is, all three internal angles are also equal to each other and are each 60°. They are regular polygons, and can therefore also be referred to as regular triangles.
   a. Isotomic conjugate
   b. A Mathematical Theory of Communication
   c. Equilateral triangle
   d. A chemical equation

34.   An _____ is a triangle that has one internal angle larger than 90°
   a. Obtuse triangle
   b. A Mathematical Theory of Communication
   c. A chemical equation
   d. Isotomic conjugate

35.   In mathematics, an algebraic group G contains a unique maximal normal solvable subgroup; and this subgroup is closed. Its identity component is called the _____ of G.

a. Composite
b. Barycentric coordinates
c. Radical
d. Block size

36. In mathematics, a _____ of a number x is a number r such that r² = x, or, in other words, a number r whose square is x. Every non-negative real number x has a unique non-negative _____, called the principal _____, which is denoted with a radical symbol as $\sqrt{x}$, or, using exponent notation, as x^(1/2). For example, the principal _____ of 9 is 3, denoted $\sqrt{9}$ = 3, because 3² = 3 × 3 = 9.
   a. Square root
   b. Multiplicative inverse
   c. Hyperbolic functions
   d. Double exponential

37. In vascular plants, the _____ is the organ of a plant body that typically lies below the surface of the soil. This is not always the case, however, since a _____ can also be aerial (that is, growing above the ground) or aerating (that is, growing up above the ground or especially above water.) Furthermore, a stem normally occurring below ground is not exceptional either
   a. 120-cell
   b. Root
   c. 2-3 heap
   d. 1-center problem

38. A _____ is the longest side of a right triangle, the side opposite of the right angle. The length of the _____ of a right triangle can be found using the Pythagorean theorem, which states that the square of the length of the _____ equals the sum of the squares of the lengths of the two other sides.

For example, if one of the other sides has a length of 3 meters and the other has a length of 4 m.

   a. Golden angle
   b. Reflection symmetry
   c. Hypotenuse
   d. Concyclic points

Chapter 9. GEOMETRY

39. In a right triangle, the cathetusoriginally from the Greek word KÎ¬θετος, plural catheti

- 1 Generally
- 2 References
- 3 See also
- 4 External links

In a wider sense, a _____ is any line falling perpendicularly on another line or a surface. Such a line is more commonly known as a surface normal.

   a. Line segment
   b. Face diagonal
   c. Central angle
   d. Cathetus

40. In mathematics, the _____ or Pythagoras' theorem is a relation in Euclidean geometry among the three sides of a right triangle. The theorem is named after the Greek mathematician Pythagoras, who by tradition is credited with its discovery and proof, although it is often argued that knowledge of the theory predates him.. The theorem is as follows:

In any right triangle, the area of the square whose side is the hypotenuse is equal to the sum of the areas of the squares whose sides are the two legs.

   a. 2-3 heap
   b. 1-center problem
   c. Pythagorean theorem
   d. 120-cell

41. In mathematics, a _____ is a statement that can be proved on the basis of explicitly stated or previously agreed assumptions.

   a. Theorem
   b. Logical value
   c. Boolean function
   d. Disjunction introduction

Chapter 10. REAL NUMBERS

1. The _____ are the set of numbers consisting of the natural numbers including 0 and their negatives. They are numbers that can be written without a fractional or decimal component, and fall within the set {... −2, −1, 0, 1, 2, ...}.
   a. A chemical equation
   b. A Mathematical Theory of Communication
   c. Integers
   d. A posteriori

2. In mathematics, the _____ of a number n is the number that, when added to n, yields zero. The _____ of n is denoted −n. For example, 7 is −7, because 7 + (−7) = 0, and the _____ of −0.3 is 0.3, because −0.3 + 0.3 = 0.
   a. Associativity
   b. Algebraic structure
   c. Arity
   d. Additive inverse

3. In mathematics, a _____ is a number which can be expressed as a ratio of two integers. Non-integer _____ s are usually written as the vulgar fraction $\frac{a}{b}$, where b is not zero. a is called the numerator, and b the denominator.
   a. Pre-algebra
   b. Minkowski distance
   c. Tally marks
   d. Rational number

4. In mathematics, an inequality is a statement about the relative size or order of two objects. For example 14 > 10, or 14 is _____ 10. The notation a > b means that a is _____ b and 'a' would be to the right of 'b' on a number line.
   a. Cauchy-Schwarz inequality
   b. Minkowski inequality
   c. FKG inequality
   d. Greater than

5. The _____ is a decimalised system of measurement. It exists in several variations, with different choices of base units, though the choice of base units does not affect its day-to-day use. Over the last two centuries, different variants have been considered the _____.
   a. 1-center problem
   b. Nonlinear system
   c. George Dantzig
   d. Metric system

Chapter 10. REAL NUMBERS

6. In mathematics, an _____ in the sense of ring theory is a subring $\mathcal{O}$ of a ring R that satisfies the conditions

    1. R is a ring which is a finite-dimensional algebra over the rational number field $\mathbb{Q}$
    2. $\mathcal{O}$ spans R over $\mathbb{Q}$, so that $\mathbb{Q}\mathcal{O} = R$, and
    3. $\mathcal{O}$ is a lattice in R.

The third condition can be stated more accurately, in terms of the extension of scalars of R to the real numbers, embedding R in a real vector space. In less formal terms, additively $\mathcal{O}$ should be a free abelian group generated by a basis for R over $\mathbb{Q}$.

The leading example is the case where R is a number field K and $\mathcal{O}$ is its ring of integers. In algebraic number theory there are examples for any K other than the rational field of proper subrings of the ring of integers that are also _____s.

a. Algebraic
b. Annihilator
c. Efficiency
d. Order

7. In mathematics the concept of a _____ generalizes notions such as 'length', 'area', and 'volume'. Informally, given some base set, a '_____' is any consistent assignment of 'sizes' to the subsets of the base set. Depending on the application, the 'size' of a subset may be interpreted as its physical size, the amount of something that lies within the subset, or the probability that some random process will yield a result within the subset.

a. Cusp
b. Congruent
c. Lattice
d. Measure

8. In mathematics, the _____s may be described informally in several different ways. The _____s include both rational numbers, such as 42 and −23/129, and irrational numbers, such as pi and the square root of two; or, a _____ can be given by an infinite decimal representation, such as 2.4871773339...., where the digits continue in some way; or, the _____s may be thought of as points on an infinitely long number line.

These descriptions of the _____s, while intuitively accessible, are not sufficiently rigorous for the purposes of pure mathematics.

64 Chapter 10. REAL NUMBERS

  a. Tally marks
  b. Pre-algebra
  c. Minkowski distance
  d. Real Number

9. In mathematics, the _____ of a real number is its numerical value without regard to its sign. So, for example, 3 is the _____ of both 3 and −3.

The _____ of a number a is denoted by | a |.

Generalizations of the _____ for real numbers occur in a wide variety of mathematical settings.

  a. Area hyperbolic functions
  b. A chemical equation
  c. Absolute value
  d. A Mathematical Theory of Communication

10. In mathematics, a _____ is a picture of a straight line in which the integers are shown as specially-marked points evenly spaced on the line. Although this image only shows the integers from -9 to 9, the line includes all real numbers, continuing 'forever' in each direction. It is often used as an aid in teaching simple addition and subtraction, especially involving negative numbers.
  a. Number system
  b. Real number
  c. Point plotting
  d. Number line

11. An _____ is a number which is involved in addition. A number being added is considered to be an _____.
  a. A posteriori
  b. Addend
  c. A chemical equation
  d. A Mathematical Theory of Communication

Chapter 10. REAL NUMBERS

12. In mathematics, the term _____ has several different important meanings:

- An _____ is an equality that remains true regardless of the values of any variables that appear within it, to distinguish it from an equality which is true under more particular conditions. For this, the 'triple bar' symbol ≡ is sometimes used.
- In algebra, an _____ or _____ element of a set S with a binary operation Â· is an element e that, when combined with any element x of S, produces that same x. That is, eÂ·x = xÂ·e = x for all x in S.
  - The _____ function from a set S to itself, often denoted id or id_S, s the function such that i = x for all x in S. This function serves as the _____ element in the set of all functions from S to itself with respect to function composition.
  - In linear algebra, the _____ matrix of size n is the n-by-n square matrix with ones on the main diagonal and zeros elsewhere. This matrix serves as the _____ with respect to matrix multiplication.

A common example of the first meaning is the trigonometric _____

$$\sin^2 \theta + \cos^2 \theta = 1$$

which is true for all real values of θ, as opposed to

$$\cos \theta = 1,$$

which is true only for some values of θ, not all. For example, the latter equation is true when $\theta = 0$, false when $\theta = 2$

The concepts of 'additive _____' and 'multiplicative _____' are central to the Peano axioms. The number 0 is the 'additive _____' for integers, real numbers, and complex numbers. For the real numbers, for all $a \in \mathbb{R}$,

$$0 + a = a,$$

$$a + 0 = a, \text{ and}$$

$$0 + 0 = 0.$$

Similarly, The number 1 is the 'multiplicative _____' for integers, real numbers, and complex numbers.

a. Identity
b. ARIA
c. Action
d. Intersection

Chapter 10. REAL NUMBERS

13. A _____ is a device for performing mathematical calculations, distinguished from a computer by having a limited problem solving ability and an interface optimized for interactive calculation rather than programming. _____s can be hardware or software, and mechanical or electronic, and are often built into devices such as PDAs or mobile phones.

Modern electronic _____s are generally small, digital, and usually inexpensive.

a. 1-center problem
b. 120-cell
c. 2-3 heap
d. Calculator

14. In mathematics, a _____ can mean either an element of the set {1, 2, 3, ...} (i.e the positive integers) or an element of the set {0, 1, 2, 3, ...} (i.e. the non-negative integers).
a. Bounded
b. FISH
c. Whole number
d. Degrees of freedom

15. _____ is the mathematical operation of scaling one number by another. It is one of the four basic operations in elementary arithmetic.

_____ is defined for whole numbers in terms of repeated addition; for example, 4 multiplied by 3 can be calculated by adding 3 copies of 4 together:

$$4 + 4 + 4 = 12.$$

_____ of rational numbers and real numbers is defined by systematic generalization of this basic idea.

a. The number 0 is even.
b. Least common multiple
c. Highest common factor
d. Multiplication

16. In abstract algebra, a field extension L /K is called _____ if every element of L is _____ over K. Field extensions which are not _____.

For example, the field extension R/Q, that is the field of real numbers as an extension of the field of rational numbers, is transcendental, while the field extensions C/R and Q

Chapter 10. REAL NUMBERS

a. Algebraic
b. Echo
c. Identity
d. Ideal

17. In mathematics, the multiplicative inverse of a number x, denoted 1/x or x^{-1}, is the number which, when multiplied by x, yields 1. The multiplicative inverse of x is also called the _____ of x.

   a. 120-cell
   b. 2-3 heap
   c. 1-center problem
   d. Reciprocal

18. In mathematics, a division is called a _____ if the divisor is zero. Such a division can be formally expressed as $\frac{a}{0}$ where a is the dividend. Whether this expression can be assigned a well-defined value depends upon the mathematical setting.

   a. 2-3 heap
   b. 120-cell
   c. 1-center problem
   d. Division by Zero

19. In algebra and computer programming, when a number or expression is both preceded and followed by a binary operation, a rule is required for which operation should be applied first; this rule is known as an _____ . From the earliest use of mathematical notation, multiplication took precedence over addition, whichever side of a number it appeared on. Thus 3 + 4 × 5 = 5 × 4 + 3 = 23.

   a. Algebraic K-theory
   b. Order of operations
   c. Isomorphism class
   d. Identity element

Chapter 11. ALGEBRA: SOLVING EQUATIONS AND PROBLEMS

1. In abstract algebra, a field extension L /K is called _____ if every element of L is _____ over K. Field extensions which are not _____.

For example, the field extension R/Q, that is the field of real numbers as an extension of the field of rational numbers, is transcendental, while the field extensions C/R and Q

   a. Echo
   b. Algebraic
   c. Identity
   d. Ideal

2. In mathematics, the _____ of a number n is the number that, when added to n, yields zero. The _____ of n is denoted −n. For example, 7 is −7, because 7 + (−7) = 0, and the _____ of −0.3 is 0.3, because −0.3 + 0.3 = 0.
   a. Algebraic structure
   b. Associativity
   c. Arity
   d. Additive inverse

3. A _____ is a device for performing mathematical calculations, distinguished from a computer by having a limited problem solving ability and an interface optimized for interactive calculation rather than programming. _____s can be hardware or software, and mechanical or electronic, and are often built into devices such as PDAs or mobile phones.

Modern electronic _____s are generally small, digital, and usually inexpensive.

   a. 1-center problem
   b. 2-3 heap
   c. 120-cell
   d. Calculator

4. In mathematics, a _____ can mean either an element of the set {1, 2, 3, ...} (i.e the positive integers) or an element of the set {0, 1, 2, 3, ...} (i.e. the non-negative integers).
   a. Degrees of freedom
   b. Bounded
   c. FISH
   d. Whole number

5. In the study of metric spaces in mathematics, there are various notions of two metrics on the same underlying space being 'the same', or _____.

Chapter 11. ALGEBRA: SOLVING EQUATIONS AND PROBLEMS 69

In the following, M will denote a non-empty set and d_1 and d_2 will denote two metrics on M.

The two metrics d_1 and d_2 are said to be topologically _____ if they generate the same topology on M.

a. A Mathematical Theory of Communication
b. A chemical equation
c. A posteriori
d. Equivalent

6. In mathematics, the term _____ has several different important meanings:

   - An _____ is an equality that remains true regardless of the values of any variables that appear within it, to distinguish it from an equality which is true under more particular conditions. For this, the 'triple bar' symbol ≡ is sometimes used.
   - In algebra, an _____ or _____ element of a set S with a binary operation Â· is an element e that, when combined with any element x of S, produces that same x. That is, eÂ·x = xÂ·e = x for all x in S.
     - The _____ function from a set S to itself, often denoted id or id_S, s the function such that i = x for all x in S. This function serves as the _____ element in the set of all functions from S to itself with respect to function composition.
     - In linear algebra, the _____ matrix of size n is the n-by-n square matrix with ones on the main diagonal and zeros elsewhere. This matrix serves as the _____ with respect to matrix multiplication.

A common example of the first meaning is the trigonometric _____

$$\sin^2 \theta + \cos^2 \theta = 1$$

which is true for all real values of θ, as opposed to

$$\cos \theta = 1,$$

which is true only for some values of θ, not all. For example, the latter equation is true when $\theta = 0$, false when $\theta = 2$

Chapter 11. ALGEBRA: SOLVING EQUATIONS AND PROBLEMS

The concepts of 'additive _____' and 'multiplicative _____' are central to the Peano axioms. The number 0 is the 'additive _____' for integers, real numbers, and complex numbers. For the real numbers, for all $a \in \mathbb{R}$,

$$0 + a = a,$$

$$a + 0 = a, \text{ and}$$

$$0 + 0 = 0.$$

Similarly, The number 1 is the 'multiplicative _____' for integers, real numbers, and complex numbers.

a. Action
b. Intersection
c. ARIA
d. Identity

7. In mathematics, and in particular in abstract algebra, distributivity is a property of binary operations that generalises the _____ law from elementary algebra.
   a. General linear group
   b. Closure with a twist
   c. Distributive
   d. Permutation

8. A _____ is one of the basic shapes of geometry: a polygon with three corners or vertices and three sides or edges which are line segments. A _____ with vertices A, B, and C is denoted ABC.

In Euclidean geometry any three non-collinear points determine a unique _____ and a unique plane.

   a. Kepler triangle
   b. 1-center problem
   c. Triangle
   d. Fuhrmann circle

9. In mathematics, _____ is a property that a binary operation can have. It means that, within an expression containing two or more of the same associative operators in a row, the order that the operations are performed does not matter as long as the sequence of the operands is not changed. That is, rearranging the parentheses in such an expression will not change its value.

Chapter 11. ALGEBRA: SOLVING EQUATIONS AND PROBLEMS

a. Unital
b. Algebraically closed
c. Associativity
d. Idempotence

10. In linear algebra, two n-by-n matrices A and B over the field K are called _____ if there exists an invertible n-by-n matrix P over K such that

$$P^{-1}AP = B.$$

One of the meanings of the term similarity transformation is such a transformation of a matrix A into a matrix B.

Similarity is an equivalence relation on the space of square matrices.

_____ matrices share many properties:

- rank
- determinant
- trace
- eigenvalues
- characteristic polynomial
- minimal polynomial
- elementary divisors

There are two reasons for these facts:

- two _____ matrices can be thought of as describing the same linear map, but with respect to different bases
- the map $X \mapsto P^{-1}XP$ is an automorphism of the associative algebra of all n-by-n matrices, as the one-object case of the above category of all matrices.

Because of this, for a given matrix A, one is interested in finding a simple 'normal form' B which is _____ to A -- the study of A then reduces to the study of the simpler matrix B.

a. Similar
b. Dense
c. Coherence
d. Blinding

11. _____ is the mathematical operation of scaling one number by another. It is one of the four basic operations in elementary arithmetic.

Chapter 11. ALGEBRA: SOLVING EQUATIONS AND PROBLEMS

_____ is defined for whole numbers in terms of repeated addition; for example, 4 multiplied by 3 can be calculated by adding 3 copies of 4 together:

$$4 + 4 + 4 = 12.$$

_____ of rational numbers and real numbers is defined by systematic generalization of this basic idea.

a. Least common multiple
b. The number 0 is even.
c. Highest common factor
d. Multiplication

12. In mathematics, a _____ is a constant multiplicative factor of a certain object. For example, in the expression $9x^2$, the _____ of x^2 is 9.

The object can be such things as a variable, a vector, a function, etc.

a. Coefficient
b. Stability radius
c. Fibonacci polynomials
d. Multivariate division algorithm

13. In mathematics, a _____ for a number x, denoted by $1/x$ or x^{-1}, is a number which when multiplied by x yields the multiplicative identity, 1. The _____ of x is also called the reciprocal of x. The _____ of a fraction p/q is q/p.

a. Double exponential
b. Hyperbolic function
c. Golden function
d. Multiplicative inverse

14. In mathematics, _____ is the problem of finding what values fulfill a condition stated as an equality. Usually, this condition involves expressions with variables, which are to be substituted by values in order for the equality to hold. More precisely, an equation involves some free variables.

a. A Mathematical Theory of Communication
b. A posteriori
c. Equation solving
d. A chemical equation

15. In arithmetic and number theory, the _____ or lowest common multiple or smallest common multiple of two integers a and b is the smallest positive integer that is a multiple of both a and b. Since it is a multiple, it can be divided by a and b without a remainder. If either a or b is 0, so that there is no such positive integer, then lc is defined to be zero.

   a. Plus-minus sign
   b. Plus and minus signs
   c. Lowest common denominator
   d. Least common multiple

Chapter 1
1. b	2. b	3. d	4. b	5. d	6. d	7. d	8. b	9. c	10. a
11. d	12. a	13. a	14. a	15. b	16. d	17. d	18. a	19. b	20. d
21. c	22. c	23. d	24. d	25. a	26. d	27. d	28. d	29. d	30. a
31. d	32. c	33. d	34. b	35. b	36. a	37. c	38. d	39. c	

Chapter 2
1. b	2. d	3. c	4. d	5. d	6. d	7. a	8. d	9. b	10. c
11. c	12. d	13. d	14. d	15. b	16. c				

Chapter 3
1. b	2. d	3. d	4. d	5. a	6. a	7. b	8. d	9. a	10. a
11. d	12. d	13. a	14. d	15. c	16. d	17. b	18. d		

Chapter 4
1. d	2. a	3. c	4. c	5. a	6. a	7. d	8. c	9. d	10. b
11. d	12. d	13. b	14. d	15. d	16. d	17. d	18. d		

Chapter 5
1. d	2. d	3. b	4. a	5. c	6. c	7. b	8. d	9. a	10. a
11. b	12. c								

Chapter 6
1. a	2. d	3. c	4. d	5. b	6. d	7. c	8. d	9. b	10. a
11. d	12. c	13. d							

Chapter 7
1. a	2. d	3. d	4. d	5. d	6. a	7. a	8. a	9. d	10. d
11. d	12. d	13. a	14. d	15. a	16. d	17. d	18. d	19. d	20. d
21. d									

Chapter 8
1. a	2. a	3. d	4. c	5. d	6. d	7. a	8. d	9. c	10. d
11. b	12. d	13. d							

Chapter 9
1. b	2. d	3. b	4. b	5. b	6. a	7. d	8. d	9. d	10. a
11. d	12. d	13. c	14. b	15. b	16. d	17. c	18. d	19. d	20. d
21. d	22. d	23. d	24. d	25. b	26. d	27. d	28. d	29. d	30. d
31. a	32. d	33. c	34. a	35. c	36. a	37. b	38. c	39. d	40. c
41. a									

Chapter 10
1. c	2. d	3. d	4. d	5. d	6. d	7. d	8. d	9. c	10. d
11. b	12. a	13. d	14. c	15. d	16. a	17. d	18. d	19. b	

ANSWER KEY

Chapter 11
1. b   2. d   3. d   4. d   5. d   6. d   7. c   8. c   9. c   10. a
11. d   12. a   13. d   14. c   15. d